Lost in Paris

A coloring tour across
the French capital

Sylvia Moritz & Rowan Ottesen

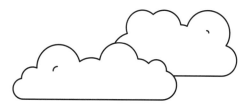

This book belongs to:

....

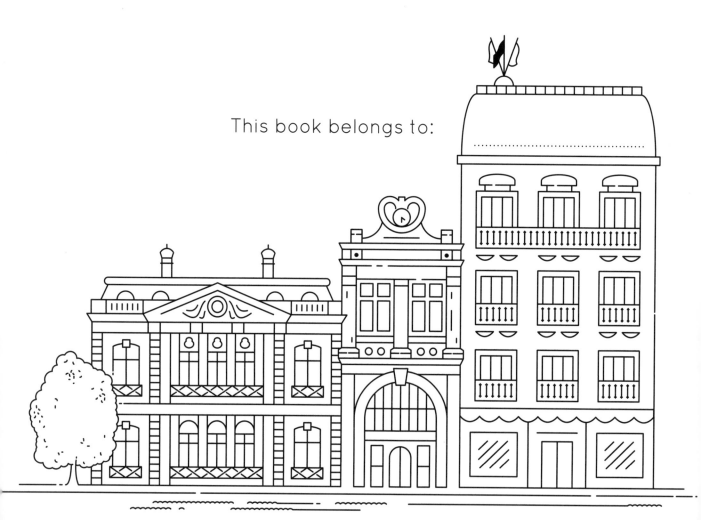

Lost in Paris

A coloring tour across
the French capital

Sylvia Moritz & Rowan Ottesen

hardie grant books

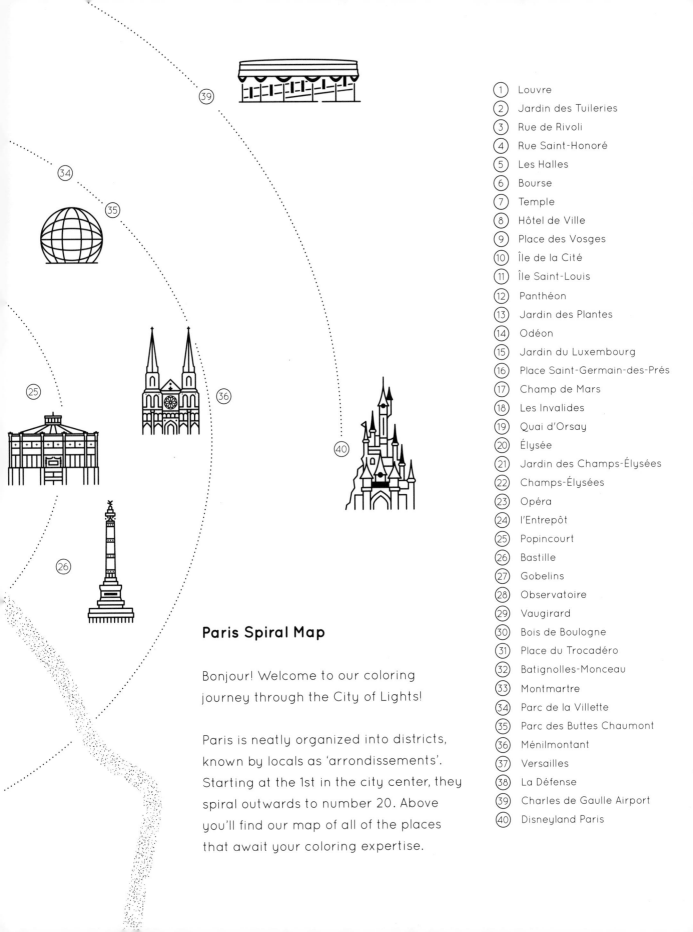

Paris Spiral Map

Bonjour! Welcome to our coloring journey through the City of Lights!

Paris is neatly organized into districts, known by locals as 'arrondissements'. Starting at the 1st in the city center, they spiral outwards to number 20. Above you'll find our map of all of the places that await your coloring expertise.

1. Louvre
2. Jardin des Tuileries
3. Rue de Rivoli
4. Rue Saint-Honoré
5. Les Halles
6. Bourse
7. Temple
8. Hôtel de Ville
9. Place des Vosges
10. Île de la Cité
11. Île Saint-Louis
12. Panthéon
13. Jardin des Plantes
14. Odéon
15. Jardin du Luxembourg
16. Place Saint-Germain-des-Prés
17. Champ de Mars
18. Les Invalides
19. Quai d'Orsay
20. Élysée
21. Jardin des Champs-Élysées
22. Champs-Élysées
23. Opéra
24. l'Entrepôt
25. Popincourt
26. Bastille
27. Gobelins
28. Observatoire
29. Vaugirard
30. Bois de Boulogne
31. Place du Trocadéro
32. Batignolles-Monceau
33. Montmartre
34. Parc de la Villette
35. Parc des Buttes Chaumont
36. Ménilmontant
37. Versailles
38. La Défense
39. Charles de Gaulle Airport
40. Disneyland Paris

Continuing to Draw the World

Every time we visited Paris in the past, a sort of spell was cast over us. We found ourselves in awe at every landmark, even if it wasn't the first time we had seen it in person. The city always inspired curiosity; it gave us the desire to wander forever, to try every food, and to go inside tourist attractions – especially if visiting hours were already over for the day.

So when we began work on our second coloring book, *Lost in Paris*, we felt that spell being cast over us again. While jotting down notes, sketching landmarks and discovering more of Paris's famous streets and beautiful parks, there were times when it was hard to resist putting down the pen, closing the laptop screen and jetting off to the City of Lights just one more time...

Although there is no substitute for the real thing, with our latest outing, we've taken great care to try to create a realistic walkthrough of Paris's incredible architecture, from the Louvre at the very heart of the city, to the Palace of Versailles outside of the city limits. We even included a Disneyland Paris spread, because even though this is an adult coloring book, there is always a little child in all of us.

Now we have laid out the canvas, it's over to you to add your own color palette to the 500+ buildings we've drawn and stitched together into our complex cityscapes. We hope you enjoy coloring each one, just as much as we enjoyed drawing them for you.

We would like to thank our publisher, Kate Pollard, for again giving us the opportunity to do what we love.

This book takes inspiration from our ongoing endeavor to intricately illustrate every city on earth. The project is called *The City Works*, and if you'd like to keep up with our progress, you can visit us at www.thecity.works or follow us @thecityworks on all social media.

We hope that you enjoy getting *Lost in Paris*, and we look forward to taking you on another urban adventure in the future.

Sylvia & Rowan

The smaller of the two Arc de Triomphes, the Arc de Triomphe du Carrousel, stands proudly opposite the glass pyramids of the Louvre. The Arc's 'big brother' can be found along the Champs-Élysées.

The Jardin des Tuileries is home to the Musée de l'Orangerie and the Jeu de Paume. Although these two buildings were constructed years apart, they are architectural twins. They face each other at the foot of the gardens.

1ST ARR

Jardin des Tuileries

Les Halles

1ST ARR

Situated in the 2nd arrondissement is the Rue des Degrés.
At only 6 meters long, this street is the shortest in Paris,
consisting of only a flight of stairs!

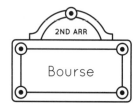

2ND ARR

Bourse

The 4th arrondissement of Paris is named after its City Hall, Hôtel de Ville. Nearby is the Centre Pompidou, an example of exoskeletal architecture, with features such as staircases, pipes and wiring on the outside of the building.

4TH ARR

Place des
Vosges

The Place des Vosges is an old square in the Marais district, lined on all four sides with beautiful symmetrical red-brick housing. One of these houses was home to famous French writer Victor Hugo.

4TH ARR

Île de la Cité

The Île de la Cité is one of a handful of small islands dotted along the River Seine. Here you'll find the Notre-Dame de Paris. The largest bell inside this famous cathedral is named Emmanuel, and weighs 13 tons.

Although its name is translated as 'new bridge', the Pont Neuf is actually one of the oldest bridges in Paris. It serves as a connector between the Île de la Cité and the left and right banks of the River Seine.

4TH ARR

Île Saint-Louis

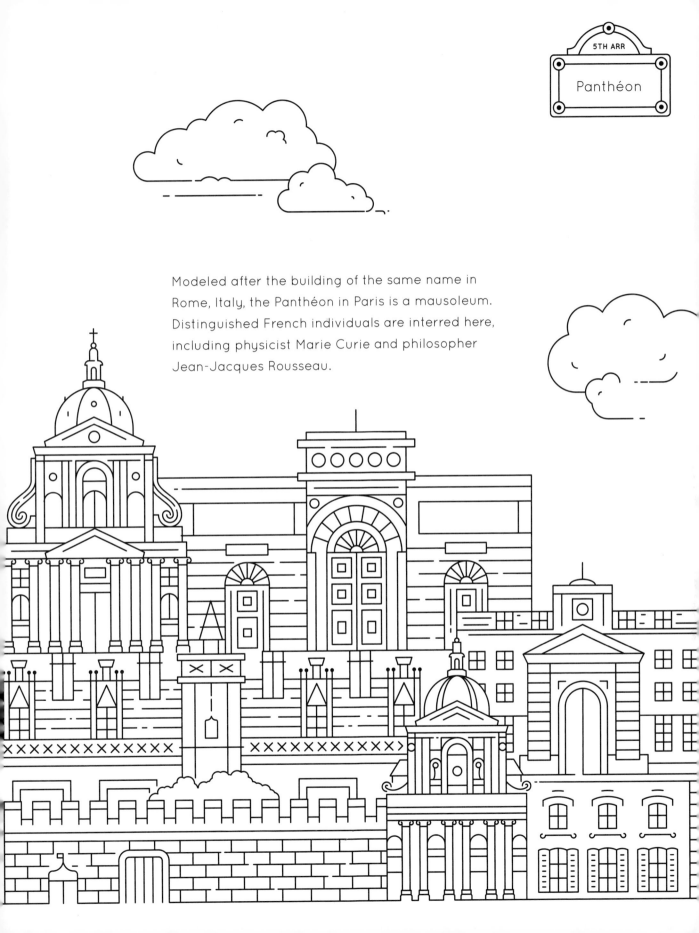

5TH ARR

Panthéon

Modeled after the building of the same name in Rome, Italy, the Panthéon in Paris is a mausoleum. Distinguished French individuals are interred here, including physicist Marie Curie and philosopher Jean-Jacques Rousseau.

Many departments of France's Natural History Museum are built in and around the Jardin des Plantes. Amongst the lush foliage of these botanical gardens, one can find museums about mineralogy, palaeontology, evolution and zoology.

5TH ARR

Jardin des
Plantes

6TH ARR

Odéon

The Luxembourg Garden is a flowery oasis in Paris's
6th arrondissement. Lined with neatly trimmed lawns,
statues, miniature lakes and fountains, it is an ideal place
for a short, peaceful walk.

Saint-Germain-des-Prés is a Parisian neighborhood renowned for its prestigious coffeehouses, such as Les Deux Magots and Café de Flore. Since their openings in the 1800s, both cafes have been famous meeting places for influential writers and intellectuals.

At the center of the Champ de Mars is the famous steel lattice monument, the Eiffel Tower. Originally built as a temporary structure for a World Fair, the (thankfully) permanent landmark is now one of the most visited in the world.

7TH ARR

Champ de Mars

7TH ARR

Les Invalides

Les Invalides are a group of buildings dedicated to French military history. At the center of the complex sits the Église Saint-Louis des Invalides, a domed chapel completely gilded with gold leaf.

At the center of the Place de la Concorde is the
Luxor Obelisk, a 3,000-year-old Egyptian column.

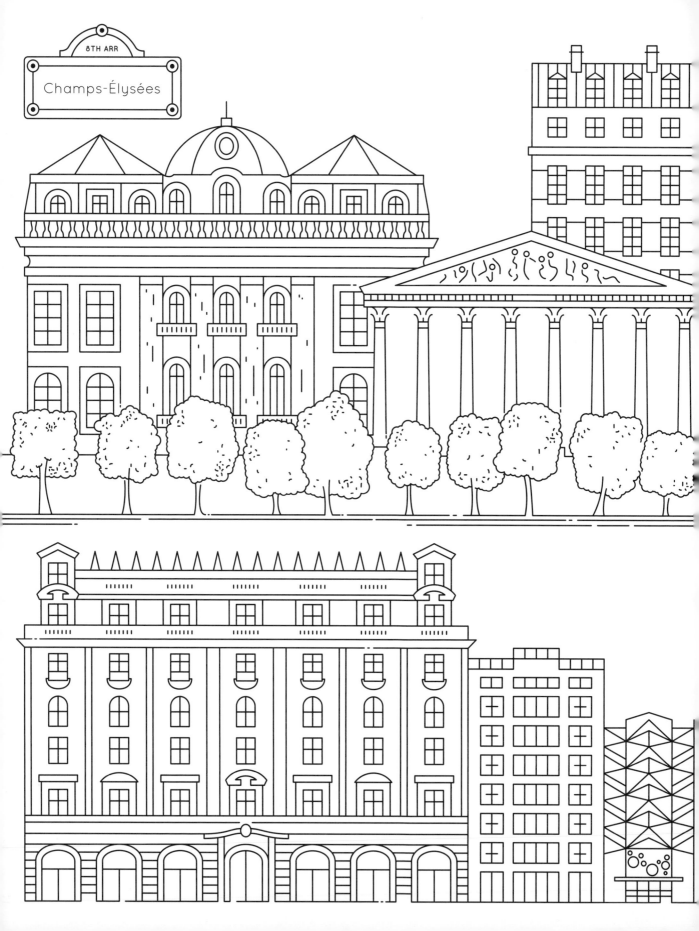

Champs-Élysées

Starting at the Luxor Obelisk, the Axe Historique is a perfectly straight line of connected Parisian landmarks. It follows the Champs Elysées past the Arc de Triomphe and ends at the Grande Arche.

9TH ARR

Opéra

The Palais Garnier is a very luxurious grand hall that has been the home of the Paris Opera for many years. Named after its architect, Charles Garnier, the building is situated in the 9th district of Paris, which is also aptly named Opéra.

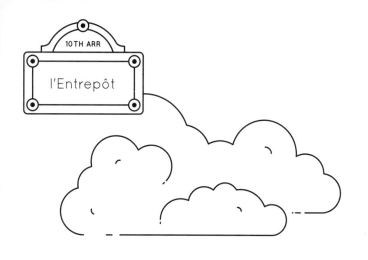

L'Entrepôt is Paris's 10th Arrondissement. Two of the city's better-known central train stations, Gare de l'Est and Gare du Nord, are located here, side by side.

Popincourt

11TH ARR

The 11th arrondissement of Paris is home to the Cirque d'Hiver, a colorful and ornate venue for musical theatre, dressage and of course, circuses.

The Place de la Bastille is a public square that marks the area where the Bastille Prison once stood, before it was stormed and subsequently destroyed during the French Revolution. The day this happened is now an annual public holiday, known as Bastille Day.

12TH ARR

Bastille

The Olympiades are a number of high-rise buildings in the
Gobelins district. Built in the early 1970s, each tower is named after
a city that has hosted the Olympic Games.

Underneath the streets of Paris are the Catacombs, an enormous network of underground tunnels, home to one of the largest ossuaries in the world. Tourists today can descend these tunnels, to witness the carefully laid remains of millions of bones.

15TH ARR

Vaugirard

Even though the Statue of Liberty was a gift from France to America, many replicas of the famous statue are dotted throughout Paris. One is located on the Île aux Cygnes, a small man-made island on the River Seine.

Place du Trocadéro

The Palais de Chaillot is a large building situated on the Place du Trocadéro, a large plaza in central Paris. Inside one can find museums about ethnology, naval history and famous French monuments. It's also an ideal spot for perfect views of the Eiffel Tower.

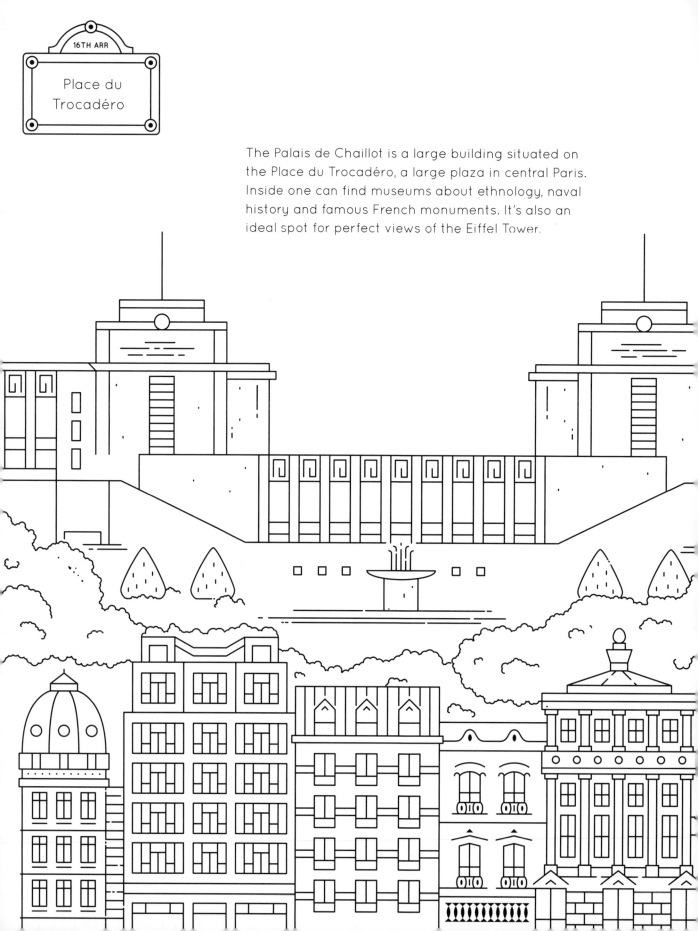

Montmartre is the highest natural point in Paris, with the Sacré-Cœur Basilica at its summit. This hillside village is also home to the Clos Montmartre, the only vineyard in Paris.

18TH ARR

Montmartre

The Parc de la Villette in the 19th arrondissement
boasts more than just beautiful trees. The grounds
are home to a variety of cultural buildings, including
a science museum, symphony hall, and a theatre, all
connected by a series of leafy walkways.

Parc de la Villette

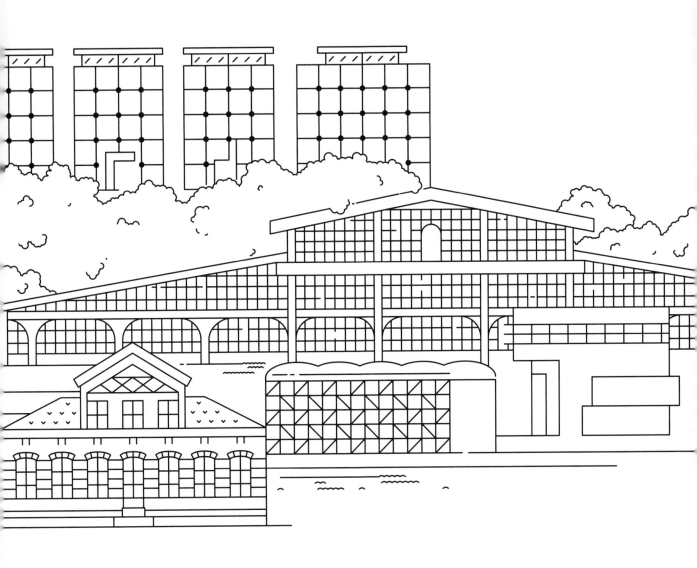

19TH ARR

Parc de
la Villette

19TH ARR

Parc des
Buttes Chaumont

20TH ARR

Ménilmontant

The Père Lachaise Cemetery, in the final outer district, is the largest in Paris. It serves as the resting place of many famous people, including the lead singer of The Doors, Jim Morrison, cabaret singer Édith Piaf and Irish playwright Oscar Wilde.

Versailles

La Défense

La Défense is a business district on the outskirts of Paris. It takes its name from a statue, La Défense de Paris, which honors the memory of the Franco-Prussian War.

La Défense

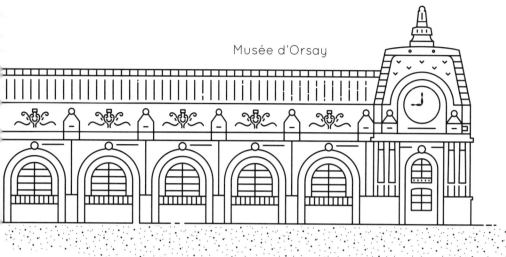

Musée d'Orsay

Arc de Triomphe

July Column

Conciergerie

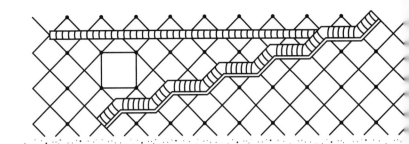

Centre Georges Pompidou

Hôtel de Ville

Petit Palais

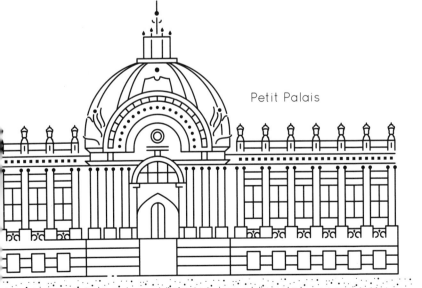

Eiffel Tower

Louvre

Le Château de la
Belle au Bois Dormant

Palais Garnier

Palais Bourbon

Musée de l'Orangerie

Les Invalides

Luxor Obelisk

Notre Dame de Paris

Sacré-Cœur Basilica

Lost in Paris by Sylvia Moritz and Rowan Ottesen

First published in 2017 by Hardie Grant Books

Hardie Grant Books (UK)
5th Floor
52-54 Southwark Street
London SE1 1UN
hardiegrant.co.uk

Hardie Grant Books (Australia)
Ground Floor, Building 1
658 Church Street
Melbourne, VIC 3121
hardiegrant.com.au

British Library Cataloguing-in-Publication Data. A catalogue record
for this book is available from the British Library.

UK ISBN: 978-1-78488-079-8
US ISBN: 978-1-78488-091-0

Publisher: Kate Pollard
Senior Editor: Kajal Mistry
Editorial Assistant: Hannah Roberts
Art Direction: Sylvia Moritz and Rowan Ottesen
Color Reproduction by p2d

Printed and bound in China by 1010

10 9 8 7 6 5 4 3 2 1